Radical Leaders

A guide for Elders and Deacons in Baptist churches

Revised Edition

Paul Beasley-Murray

Baptist Union
of Great Britain

www.baptist.org.uk

2005

Published on behalf of The Baptist Union of Great Britain
by Nigel Lynn Publishing & Marketing Ltd
106 High Street, Milton under Wychwood, Chipping Norton
Oxfordshire, OX7 6ET, United Kingdom

The Baptist Union of Great Britain
Baptist House, 129 Broadway, Didcot
Oxfordshire, OX11 8RT, United Kingdom

First published 1997
Second edition published 2005

British Library Cataloguing in Publication Data
Data available

ISBN   0 901472 63 8

1 3 5 7 9 10 8 6 4 2

Cover design by Wheeler & Porter Ltd, Banbury
Printed in the United Kingdom
on acid-free paper by
The Alden Group, Oxford

CONTENTS

THE AUTHOR

Paul Beasley-Murray is currently the senior minister of Central Baptist Church, Victoria Road South, Chelmsford, Essex. After serving for two years with the Baptist Missionary Society in Congo (Zaire), he pastored the Baptist church in Altrincham, Cheshire for thirteen years, before becoming Principal of Spurgeon's College, London, from 1986 to 1992.

He is also the Chair of 'Ministry Today', which aims to 'provide a supportive resource for all in pastoral leadership so that they may not only survive, but also grow and develop, becoming more effective in the ministry to which Christ has called them',and he is the General Editor of the journal *Ministry Today*.

A prolific author, he has written a number of books and booklets for Baptist Publications, which together now form the *Radical* series of publications:

Radical Believers: the Baptist way of being the church
Radical Disciples: a course for new Christians preparing for Baptism
Radical Leaders: a guide for elders and deacons
Happy Ever After? A 'radical' workbook for couples preparing for marriage

He is also preparing a new book on leadership in the local church which will be published by IVP (ISBN 978 1 84474 085 4).

Dedication

In appreciation of all those deacons who have served with me in my churches in Altrincham and in Chelmsford. To a large degree I am what I am because of them.

Preface to the Second Edition

It has been gratifying to see the way in which *Radical Leaders* has become accepted as the basic textbook for many leaders in Baptist churches. In my own church every new deacon receives a copy of *Radical Leaders*!

The changes made to this second edition are minimal, and for the most part simply reflect structural changes which have taken place in the life of the Baptist Union (e.g. 'general superintendents' are now called 'regional ministers').

Unless otherwise specified, Biblical quotations are from the NRSV.

INTRODUCTION

I have become a servant according to the gift of God's grace.

Finding our roots

Radical Believers, *Radical Disciples*, now *Radical Leaders*. Quite unintentionally a series has developed. *Radical Believers* sought to root in the New Testament the Baptist way of being the church. *Radical Disciples* is a baptismal course which looks at what the Scriptures have to say on various aspects of the Christian life. And now *Radical Leaders*. Here again we are seeking to root the distinctive role of Christian leadership within the New Testament.

Let me make it clear from the start. Baptist churches today are undoubtedly different from the churches we encounter within the pages of the New Testament. Life has moved on, and conditions are so very different. Most Baptist churches, for instance, have their own building. Many Baptist churches have trained pastors. We have hymn books, overhead projectors and now PowerPoint® to help us in our worship. There is no way in which we can re-create a New Testament church. And yet I believe that there are fundamental principles of church life to be found in the New Testament which are still of great relevance. And what is true of church life in general, is true too of Christian leadership in particular. Yes, I freely accept that there is no divine blueprint on which every aspect of church life and Christian leadership can be patterned. The church constitutions and rules by which we govern our life would no doubt amaze the Apostle Paul. And yet in spite of all the complexities of modern church life, people are still people. The emotions and aspirations which bubble beneath the surface of every church are not peculiar to our day, but rather would have been familiar to the apostles of old. Precisely because the human condition has not fundamentally changed, the teaching of the New Testament still speaks into our situation.

The conviction therefore underlying this guide to Christian leadership is that we need to root our life together in the New Testament. Hence the adjective 'radical'. 'Radical' does not necessarily imply that every deacon or elder votes Labour and flies the Red Flag. Nor for that matter that every deacon or elder sports a straggly beard, wears open sandals even in the depths of winter and belongs to some freakish anti-technological group. No, the English word 'radical' is derived from the Latin word *radix* which means 'root'. Radical leaders are those who root their practice and style of leadership in principles to be discerned in the pages of the New Testament.

The challenge of diversity

One of the difficulties I face in writing this guide to leadership is the differences which result from the size of churches. For instance, the dynamics of being a leader in a church with thirty five members are very different from being a leader in a church with 350 members—and all the more so if the church with thirty five members is not able to support a pastor. At every stage it will be necessary for readers to contextualise what I am saying, so that it becomes relevant to you and your church.

A further difficulty in writing this guide for 'lay' leaders within Baptist churches is that of terminology. The very fact that I have had to put the word 'lay' in inverted commas is one sign of the difficulty. For in certain circles the word 'lay' is the ecclesiastical equivalent of a non-politically correct word. The fact is that 'clergy' (what an abominable word!) as much as 'non-clergy' belong to the people (Greek *laos*) of God. Indeed, bearing in mind the Greek term *laos*, it could be maintained that all of us, ordained and non-ordained, belong to God's 'laity' (1 Peter 2.9)! So what alternative generic term do we find for 'lay' leaders? Is this a book for the non-ordained? The very term 'non-ordained' is something of a put-down and suggests something is missing! Is this a book for leaders who are not in 'full-time' service? Again the term is unhelpful—it suggests that the world of work is of little value in the sight of God.

This book, then, is for deacons and elders. But that description again begs a question. What's the difference between deacons and elders? The question becomes complicated since the majority of Baptist churches do not have elders. True, there was a time when one stream of Baptist life did have elders and deacons, but by and large the office of elder died out. Since the 1960s the office of elder has been re-introduced into a good number of Baptist churches, largely as a result of charismatic renewal. In such churches elders are seen as having a leadership role in the spiritual and pastoral affairs of the church, while the deacons are seen as responsible for the more practical affairs of the church's life. In practice, however, the distinction between the 'spiritual' and the 'practical' cannot easily be maintained—the handling of money, for instance, normally seen as a diaconal responsibility, calls for a high degree of spirituality! On the other hand, it is true to say that in some churches where there are no elders, although in theory the deacons are responsible for overseeing both the spiritual and practical affairs of the church's life, time and again the practical concerns override the spiritual ones.

What does the New Testament have to say about this? Very little! As we shall see in the next chapter, although it is clear that in the church at Ephesus there were both elders and deacons (see 1 Timothy 3.1–13), the pattern does not appear to have been repeated at Corinth or at Jerusalem. Furthermore, nobody can be sure of the difference in role between elders and deacons at Ephesus—the one clear distinguishing feature between elders (otherwise known as bishops) is that they had to be gifted to teach (1 Timothy 3.2). Add to all this the fact that the term 'elder' reflects a society where middle age did not exist ('young' men were deemed to be under forty, while anybody over forty was deemed to be an old man!), and the re-introduction of the term becomes, to my way of thinking, all the more strange. The fact is that there is no one clear blueprint for leadership within the New Testament—but there are simply principles for leadership.

But to return to my present dilemma. It is not my brief to bring about a change of terminology in Baptist churches. If you only have deacons in your church, God bless you! If you have both deacons and elders in your church, God bless you too! My concern is to address the issue of leadership. Yet to speak in terms of 'elders and deacons' all the time can be cumbersome. I therefore propose to use the term 'leaders'. 'Leaders' in this context includes both elders and deacons. 'Leaders' meetings' refers both to elders' meetings and deacons' meetings. Pastors, of course, are also leaders—indeed, they are called to spearhead the mission and ministry of the church by acting as the leaders of the leaders. However, this book is not in the first place intended for pastors.

The ministry of all and the leadership of some

Amidst all the diversity to be found in Baptist churches, Baptists are at one in their belief in the ministry of all believers. A number of Bible passages could be cited supporting this doctrine, but the chapter which particularly comes to mind is 1 Corinthians 12. Here Paul develops the picture of the church as a body. God, says Paul, has so designed the body that the involvement of every person with his or her special gift is necessary for the proper functioning of the community. Every member has a unique role to play. Yes, there are particular leadership roles give by God to certain individuals, but these individuals do not have a monopoly of the Holy Spirit. For bests results, all God's people are needed, pulling together.

One particular expression of the ministry of all believers is to be found in the Baptist church meeting. Baptists believe that it is as they come together in the name of the Lord Jesus that God makes his will known for their life together. The church meeting is the ultimate authority in the life of any Baptist church. However, this is not to deny the place of leadership in the context of the church meeting. In the words of Frank Cooke, a former President of the Baptist Union,

> The church meeting is not a papal audience nor is it a 'Parliamentary party battle ground'. It is the family of God rejoicing in its response to visionary and loving leadership, in worship, in prayer, and in mutual submission to one another.

(For a more detailed consideration of the church meeting, please see chapter 6 of *Radical Believers*: 'Living under the Lordship of Christ—Authority among Baptists').

It is, however, important to point out that although ecclesiologically the church meeting has ultimate authority with regard to any decisions taken by the church, when it comes to the law the church's leaders are held responsible for the church's decisions. In legal terms the church's leaders (whether they be called ministers, elders or deacons) are the 'charity trustees', who in turn are subject to the general requirements of charity law. This is a complex area of law, which affects not only the church's management of property but also its accounting procedures. In this respect leaders are advised to get hold of a copy of *Guidelines to the Charities Act 1993* prepared by the Baptist Union Corporation Ltd, to whom further queries may be addressed.

High calling but high stress

It's a wonderful privilege to be elected a leader in the church of God. The church in its wisdom has expressed its confidence in you and in the gifts that God has given you. You have been given a special opportunity to serve God and your fellow church members as you help give shape and direction to your church. For the next few years you will be at the very heart of the church's life. There will be little that you will not know. Assuming that you have a pastor, you will probably be able to draw alongside your pastor in a way which would not normally be possible to other people. From time to time your involvement as a leader may expose you to a degree of pain; for inevitably as a leader you will experience perhaps more than most some of the heartaches of the church family to which you belong. Yet almost certainly the joys will outweigh the sorrows. Hopefully your very experience of working with other church leaders will prove to be a catalyst to your own spiritual growth.

Yet there is also a considerable responsibility in being a leader. The spiritual vitality of any church, for instance, is to a large extent dependent on its leaders. Or to put it in personal terms, the success of your church's mission and ministry is not just dependent upon your pastor, but rather is equally dependent upon the vision and dedication which you and your fellow leaders possess. Needless to say, if your church has no pastor, then your church is even more dependent upon the spiritual calibre of its leaders. It's an awesome and challenging responsibility to be elected a deacon.

It's also a time-consuming calling. The fact is that there is far more to being a leader than simply attending a leaders' meeting every now and again. For along with your normal commitments as a church member—and one would normally assume that this included regular attendance at all the main worship services and church meetings and whatever other core activities your church might feel it right to run—there is a host of other responsibilities which become now incumbent upon you. In this guide we shall seek to explore what some of these responsibilities involve. For leaders who also have responsibilities at work and at home, balancing all these conflicting interests is no easy thing. In a very real sense it is costly being a leader. But then did not David say: 'I will not offer to the Lord that which costs me nothing' (2 Samuel 24.24)?

BIBLICAL PATTERNS FOR LEADERSHIP

All scripture is inspired by God and is useful for teaching, for reproof, for correction, and for training in righteousness, so that everyone who belongs to God may be proficient, equipped for every good work.

2 Timothy 3.16,17

Leadership is a gift

All God's people are called to serve, but not all are called to lead. As Paul makes clear in 1 Corinthians 12, God gives many and various gifts, most of which relate to ministry in general. Some, however, relate to the ministry of leadership in particular.

In 1 Corinthians 12.8, for instance, Paul refers to 'those with gifts of administration' (NIV), or more accurately, those with gifts of 'leadership' (NRSV). The underlying Greek noun literally means 'helmsmanship'. It was a term often used metaphorically in Greek literature of the art of government: the statesman guiding the 'ship of state'. Here in 1 Corinthians 12 the ship in question is the church. Within the context of every-member ministry there are those specially gifted to 'direct' (GNB) the church in its worship, mission and ministry.

The ministry of leadership appears also in Paul's list of the gifts of the Spirit in Romans 12.8: 'If it is leadership, then govern diligently' (NIV, similarly NRSV), or as the GNB translates: 'Whoever has authority should work hard'. It is true that in some older English versions a different translation is found: for instance, the RSV translates the phrase, 'he who gives aid, with zeal'. In fact the underlying Greek verb can mean both 'to lead' and 'to care for'. However, rather than seeking to make distinctions between the two meanings, it is more helpful to note how the two meanings may interrelate: leadership within a church context is not about the exercise of power, but rather about the exercise of care.

The concept of leadership is also present in the list of spiritual gifts in Ephesians 4.11,12 where Paul mentions the office of the pastor-teacher. Like all the other offices, in the first place the emphasis is upon the 'enabling' aspect of this ministry—pastor-teachers enable the people of God to fulfil their various ministries. However, the actual term 'pastor' also carried clear overtones of leadership, for in the ancient world the word 'pastor' or 'shepherd' was often used as a synonym for a 'leader' or a 'king'.

Leadership is a gift for women too

The New Testament teaches that the Spirit gives his gifts irrespective of gender (Acts 2.17–18). Although certain cultural situations might limit leadership to men (see 1 Corinthians 11.3–16;14.33–36; 1 Timothy 2.11–15) in principle there is no Scriptural reason why women should not be in leadership. In the church at Rome, for instance, women as well as men took the lead: Phoebe was a deacon (Romans 16.1–2), Prisca was a teacher (Romans 16.3) and Junia was even an apostle (Romans 16.7). From Acts 21.9 (see also Acts 2.17–18) we learn that women were also prophets.

There is therefore no reason why suitably gifted women may not share the leadership with men in today's church. The long presumed superiority of male over against female no longer exists in Christ (Galatians 3.28).

Leadership is always shared

The churches of the New Testament always enjoyed shared ministry. For example, the leadership of the church at Antioch was in the hands of a group of 'prophets and teachers' (Acts 13.1). In Asia Minor Paul and Barnabas appointed 'elders' in each church. (Acts 14.23). The leadership of the Jerusalem church was made up of 'apostles and elders' (Acts 15.23). The church at Philippi had 'bishops' and 'deacons' (Philippians 1.1).

It is in the context of shared ministry and shared leadership that pastors are called to exercise their specialist ministry. This specialist ministry will normally involve acting as the leader of the leaders—just as in the Jerusalem church James was clearly the 'presiding elder' (see Acts 15).

Patterns of leadership vary from church to church

There was no set pattern of leadership in the New Testament churches. For instance:

- At Philippi there were 'bishops' and 'deacons' (see Philippians 1.1), but we do not know what their particular tasks involved. The name 'deacon', which comes from the Greek word for 'servant' (*diakonos*), implies that the deacons in Philippi helped the 'bishops' (Greek *episkopoi*, which literally means 'overseers'), but no more can be deduced.
- At Ephesus, where Timothy exercised a key pastoral role, there were 'bishops' (sometimes called 'elders') and 'deacons'; but apart from the fact that bishops had to be 'apt teachers' (1 Timothy 3.2), nothing is said about their differing roles—Paul was more concerned with their quality of personal life rather than with their role in church life.
- At Lystra, Iconium and Pisidian Antioch, Paul and Barnabas appointed 'elders' in each church (Acts 14.23), but nothing is said about deacons.
- Paul commended to the church at Rome 'our sister Phoebe, a deacon of the church at Cenchreae' (Romans 16.1). Phoebe was a lady of

some means, because she is described as 'a benefactor of many and of myself as well' (Romans 16.2), but to what extent her generosity was linked with her official role in the church is uncertain.

- At Jerusalem there were 'apostles and elders '(see Acts 15), but were there also 'deacons' in the Jerusalem church? Traditionally Baptists on the basis of Acts 6.1–6 have answered 'Yes', and have argued that the 'seven men of good standing, full of the Spirit and of wisdom' were deacons, who freed the apostles for their particular ministry of 'prayer and serving the word' by seeing to the pastoral problem posed by widows in the church. However, nowhere is it specifically said that these men were deacons. True, they were called to 'serve tables'—whatever that particular phrase might mean—but the use of the verb *diakonein* from which the noun *diakonos* comes, does not mean they necessarily filled the office of deacon—it simply means that they 'served' the church by solving a particular problem, which in turn involved caring for the widows. Certainly nowhere else in Acts do we hear of deacons in the Jerusalem church.

Leadership is always servant-leadership

On a number of occasions Jesus emphasised the necessity of the servant role if a person would be a leader. So when James and John asked if they might sit at his right and left hand in glory, Jesus replied: 'You know that among the Gentiles those whom they recognize as rulers lord it over them, and their great ones are tyrants over them. But it is not so among you; but whoever wishes to become great among you must be your servant, and whoever wishes to be first among you must be slave of all' (Mark 10.42–44; Matthew 20.25–27; see also Luke 22.24–26).

Such teaching about servant ministry seems to have been a constant theme of Jesus. For on another occasion when his disciples were arguing as to who was the greatest, Jesus said: 'Whoever wants to be first must be last of all and servant of all' (Mark 9.35; Luke 9.48). Matthew 23 is a salutary chapter for any leader to read, for there Jesus denounces the religious leaders of his day. He condemns those who 'love to have the place of honour', who 'love to be called rabbi'. 'The greatest among you will be your servant'. There is no room for pride in the heart of any Christian leader.

Jesus not only taught servant ministry, he also lived out of the life of a servant. Having washed his disciples' feet, he said: 'I have set you an example, that you also should do as I have done to you' (John 13.15). Christian leadership is always servant-leadership.

Servant-leadership is always non-coercive

Christian leadership is always a servant ministry which leaves people free to accept or not to accept its direction. It can never force others to do something over which they are basically unhappy. There is a difference between leadership and 'lordship' (see 1 Peter 5.2–3).

Leaders may have authority (see 1 Thessalonians 5.12 and Hebrews 13.17), but they can never be authoritarian. Christian leadership exhorts, rather than coerces (see 1 Timothy 5.1). Servant leadership is never from 'above', it is always from 'below'. This is brought out by Paul in 1 Corinthians 16.15–16: 'You know that members of the household of Stephanas ... have devoted themselves to the service of the saints; I urge you to put yourselves at the service of such people'.

Servant-leadership is always accountable to the church

Although leaders are accountable to God (see Galatians 1.1; Hebrews 13.17), they are also accountable to the church, which has recognised their calling and set them apart for service (Acts 13.1–3; 14.27). Accountability, however, does not rob leaders of their authority. Rightly understood, the church in appointing its leaders has delegated to them authority, authority which the leaders are free to exercise until the church withdraws its recognition of them. There is an element of tension here. On the one hand, any church meeting would need to think hard and long before overturning a unanimous recommendation from their leaders with regard, for instance, to its budget proposals for the forthcoming year. On the other hand, leaders are not infallible. The church meeting is the right place for testing all major proposals regarding church life.

APPOINTING LEADERS TODAY: JERUSALEM REVISITED

'Select from among yourselves seven men of good standing, full of the Spirit and of wisdom, whom we may appoint to this task, while we, for our part, will devote ourselves to prayer and to serving the word'. What they said pleased the whole community, and they chose Stephen, a man of faith and the Holy Spirit, together with Philip, Prochorus, Nicanor, Timon, Parmenas, and Nicolaus ... They had these men stand before the apostles, who prayed and laid their hands on them. The word of God continued to spread; the number of disciples increased greatly ...'

Acts 6.3–7a

This guide to leadership in the local church is written primarily for people who are already leaders. Yet there may well be some readers who are perhaps considering allowing their names to go forward for election as leaders. Furthermore, from time to time every leadership team has to face the issue of renewing the team and finding new colleagues. For this reason it seems sensible to look at the process of appointing leaders in the local church—and to do so in part through focussing on how the Seven were appointed to serve in the Jerusalem church.

Wanted: leaders 'full of the Spirit and of wisdom'

It is not by chance that the apostles list spirituality before ability. Clearly ability is important for those who lead God's people, but at the end of the day it is not all-important. In the first place, leaders are to be 'full of the Spirit', men and women who are on fire for God because God's Spirit has invaded their lives. They are to be people 'of good standing' (Acts 6.3)—people liked and respected by the church and the community at large.

A similar emphasis is found in 1 Timothy 3.1–13, where Paul lists the qualities necessary for those aspiring to leadership in the church at Ephesus. The emphasis there is on 'graces' rather than 'gifts'. Almost without exception Paul tells us nothing of what leaders might be expected to do—rather he writes of what leaders are expected to *be*. 'A bishop must be above reproach (1 Timothy 3.2); 'If they prove themselves blameless, let them serve as deacons' (1 Timothy 3.10). Leaders must be 'well-thought of by outsiders' (1 Timothy 3.7). If leaders are to be effective they must in the first place live lives that reflect the King whom they serve. 'Power', 'love' and 'self-discipline' are all marks of a spiritual leader (2 Timothy 1.6).

Wanted: leaders with proven qualities

Some Baptist churches today state that leaders have to be over 21—or even over 25—years of age before they can serve on the leadership team. One could argue that such restrictions are out-dated in a society when 18 is generally acknowledged to mark the formal point of transition into adult life. Yet even such an argument misses the point: for when members elect deacons, they are hopefully looking not to elect people of a certain age, but rather people who have begun to display gifts of leadership in the context of the church's worship, ministry and mission.. As Paul made clear to Timothy, age should not be an issue (2 Timothy 4.10). What counts is spiritual maturity (1 Timothy 3.6).

Other churches limit eligibility to those who have been in membership for a year or more. However, in an increasingly mobile society in which people can move all over the country for reasons of work, such a restriction is limiting. On the other hand, for the purposes of 'testing' (1 Timothy 3.10) some kind of familiarisation process is necessary. Undue haste is certainly to be avoided (2 Timothy 5.22). So does one go for a limited time restriction of say six months, or does one leave the question of suitability and timing to the discernment of the members?

Yet other churches restrict the leadership to members who have been baptised as believers. This, of course, is the only option where closed membership is practised. Yet strangely a number of 'open membership' Baptist churches have similar restrictions: for although they may welcome into membership people who have not been baptised as believers (normally unbaptised members who have already been in good standing with another church), they are not prepared to allow such people into leadership. The inevitable outcome is that those members who have not been baptised as believers are made to feel second class—and the church is not able to take advantage of all the gifts represented in the fellowship. It is not as if such members would necessarily make the church less 'Baptist'—the very fact they have become a member of a Baptist church shows that, at the very least, they are in sympathy with the practice of believers' baptism. If a safeguard is required, then surely it would be sufficient to state that two-thirds of deacons be baptised believers?

Wanted: leaders enjoying healthy relationships

Leaders lead by example in every area of their lives. The church needs to model healthy patterns of relating, and whilst growth in relationship is an on-going process leaders need to demonstrate the reality of this in their personal lives. The quality of their personal relationships is very often a mirror of the calibre of their relationships with God. If married, both partners need to be secure in their relationship with one another, and share a commitment to service for the Lord. The supporting spouse has a key role to play. Disunity in this area will very likely affect the marriage at some level with the potential for unhelpful repercussions. Although the importance of healthy relationships does not receive a mention in Acts 6, Paul certainly highlights the importance of family stability (1 Timothy 3.2,4–5,12).

Wanted: seven—or more?

The church at Jerusalem limited the number of those to be elected as leaders to seven. On the other hand, there were already twelve apostles! Frankly, there is no number which is normative for us today. Everything depends on the size of the church. For some churches seven leaders might be too many, for others twelve might not be sufficient. According to some secular studies in leadership 5% of any given group have leadership qualities!

The nomination process

In the church at Jerusalem the selection of the Seven was very much in the hands of the church as a whole (Acts 6.3). Likewise today it is important for church members to be able to play a full part in the process of nominating potential deacons.

But leaders are church members too. There is therefore no reason why leaders, in their capacity as church members, should have nothing to do with the nomination process. Indeed, in their capacity as leaders, it surely also makes sense for them to give thought on how they can encourage the next generation of leaders to come forward and develop. Just as Barnabas identified the potential in Paul and then gave him opportunities to develop that potential (Acts 11.25,26), leaders today need to identify those who have the potential for leadership and give them opportunities to develop. Provided no restrictions are placed on the membership in general, there is a lot to be said for the subject of future leaders to be an item on the agenda of a leaders' meeting, although care needs to be taken that this doesn't become manipulative.

The method of election

Unlike the world of politics, leadership elections in the church normally require potential leaders to gain a minimum of 50% of the vote in order to be elected. If the Spirit is guiding his people, one should expect at least half those voting to sense his direction. Unfortunately sometimes difficulties arise, particularly when there are many more people nominated than there are places. For when there is a large number of candidates, votes tend to get split so that only one or two may be able to get 50% of the vote, with the result that there may well still be some vacancies on the leadership team. One way of getting around this difficulty is to allow every member to have as many votes as there are candidates: for example, if there are four vacancies and seven candidates, then everybody is allowed to vote for as many of the seven that they believe have been gifted by God for leadership. Provided they all have at least 50% of the votes, the four with the most votes are then elected. The process may seem a little like Alice-in-Wonderland, but it actually works!

The welcoming of new leaders

Church leaders are elected at a church meeting. It is, however, customary for leaders to be publicly welcomed into office at a subsequent celebration of the Lord's Supper. On such an occasion it is surely good to follow the custom of the Jerusalem church and to combine that welcome with prayer and with the laying-on of hands (Acts 6.6). In New Testament times such a ceremony had primarily God's blessing in view, but probably was also carried out with a view to delegating authority to enable the leaders to discharge their duties in the name of the church (see also Acts 13.3; 1 Timothy 4.14; 2 Timothy 1.6). In today's church it is equally important that proper recognition is given to the church's leadership—and that the church is encouraged 'to trust them, pray for them, and at all times to help them in the Lord'.

Setting apart for a period

Clearly in Acts 6 the Seven were appointed to a particular task; however, there is nothing to indicate that it was time limited. On the other hand, when Paul and Barnabas were 'set apart' , they were appointed for a very specific piece of missionary service (Acts 13.1–3). Similarly today leaders in most churches are appointed to serve for a particular period—normally three years, with an option to serve a further term. In some larger churches there is a limit to the number of times a leader may serve consecutively. In such cases leaders have to take a so-called 'sabbatical' and stand down for a year after, say, two terms. There is a lot to be said for that practice, in so far as it encourages new 'blood' onto the leadership team. However, the term 'sabbatical' is unhelpful: for it implies that leaders, after having stood down for a year, automatically allow their names to go forward for re-election. But this is not necessarily healthy, either for the individual or for the church.

Right structures lead to growth

One final point before we leave the Jerusalem church: with the appointment of the Seven and the apostles freed for their particular ministry, 'the number of the disciples increased greatly' (Acts 6.7). Rightly understood, leadership structures are not some bureaucratic necessity; rather they are the means by which church growth is fostered.

RELATIONSHIPS ARE VITAL

'This is my commandment, that you love one another as I have loved you. No one has greater love than this, to lay down one's life for one's friends.'

John 15.12–13

Relationships are the key to the life of any church. A church where people do not get on with one another, where members criticise one another and maybe even play power games with one another, is a travesty of a church. If Christians can't love one another, then why should the world take any notice of them? How can we expect people to believe in the love of God when a church fails to live out this love?

In particular, relationships are the key to the life of a Baptist church. When in a Baptist church we welcome new members into fellowship, we are in fact entering into a dynamic covenant relationship with one another—a relationship in which we commit ourselves not only to work together to extend Christ's Kingdom, but also to love one another and stand by one another whatever the cost.

It is in this context that relationships between the church's leaders are so vital. For in a very real sense, the leaders set the pattern for the church's life together. If the leaders are united, then the fellowship is likely to be united. But if the leadership team is basically made up of a bunch of rugged individualists, then the church in turn is likely to reflect that same individualism. In terms of relationships the leadership team effectively sets the pace.

Inevitably relationships develop as leaders come together on a regular basis to face the everyday challenges of church life. And yet there is a limit to which relationships can develop when the pace and structure of leadership meetings is constantly dictated by the pressing concerns of a full agenda. Relationships are best nurtured in less structured and more relaxed settings. For this reason many churches have found it helpful to spend an occasional Saturday morning together, when the normal agenda may be put to one side and time given to lengthy discussions about one or two central concerns. Yet other churches prefer to devote the whole of a Saturday to an 'Awayday', which can provide a good opportunity for an in-depth look ahead soon after new leaders join the team. Better still, is to go away for a weekend together. Admittedly this is a costly exercise, both in terms of finance and time, but experience proves time and again that the investment pays enormous dividends. For in a weekend a depth of relationship can come about which otherwise might takes years to achieve.

Committed to one another

For the sake of the well-being of the church it is crucial that the leadership team does not view itself in secular terms as some kind of board of management, but rather as a group of brothers and sisters committed to one another. In a sense the leadership team is akin to a fellowship group, whose members give each other the right to call one another for help and support at any time. One of the disciplines of being part of the leadership team is giving priority to all leadership team meetings. Except in cases of legitimate mitigating circumstances all leaders will be present—and on time! Another discipline is keeping anything that is shared in the meeting strictly confidential, unless clear permission is given to inform others. Leaders need to be trustworthy (see Proverbs 11.13). Those who are tempted to gossip should make Psalm 141.3 their prayer: 'Set a guard over my mouth, O Lord; keep watch over the door of my lips'.

Loyal to one another

Commitment to one anotherness means that leaders should never criticise one another to others. Loyalty is paramount. Leaders should never let people play one leader off against the other, rather they should always support one another publicly. If there are grounds for criticism, then the criticism needs to be expressed face to face—ideally on a one to one basis, although there may be occasions when the criticism needs to surface in the leadership team meeting as a whole.

The practice of corporate responsibility is another expression of loyalty to one another. Once the leadership team has made a decision, then in public all the members abide by that decision. The only exception is when leaders in all good conscience feel that they cannot go along with the others and must make their differing viewpoint known at the church meeting: however, even then that difference should not be expressed unless at a previous leaders' meeting due notice has been given to the other leaders.

Speaking the truth in love to one another

At all times the 'truth needs to be spoken in love'. It is never good to allow problems to fester. It has been said that 'Today's niggle could be tomorrow's resentment, and next week's breakdown', but honesty always needs to be combined with love. Frankness should always be tempered with consideration for the well-being of the other. Inevitably, there will be differences of viewpoint. But often the sharing of differences proves to be a learning experience for the whole group. Indeed, leadership teams are normally the stronger when differences of outlook and personality are present. As Proverbs 27.17 puts it: 'Iron sharpens iron, and one person sharpens the wits of another'. In the clash of debate we can learn much from one another.

Speaking the truth in love is often far from easy. It can be difficult to express criticism face to face. And yet for the sake of the church, as indeed for the well-being of the team, concerns must not be suppressed. The expression of such criticisms or concerns need not, however, be always done in a confrontational manner. often a carefully phrased question can have the same effect.

Encouraging one another

Few people remain on a perpetual even keel. Rather, all of us have our ups and downs, and therefore all of us need a brother or sister to speak a word of encouragement into our lives. Hence the injunction of Paul to 'encourage one another and build one another up' (1 Thessalonians 5.11).

Leaders in particular need to encourage one another. For there are times when leadership can be a painful and difficult business—not least when certain members may misunderstand or mistrust the motives behind some of the proposals of the leadership team. Particularly when change is in the air, the moment leaders raise their heads above the parapet with a view to advancing in one direction or another, that moment they can become the target for snipers. When the flak is flying, strength can be drawn from mutual encouragement.

Welcoming one another

Hospitality helps relationships develop. Hopefully leaders and their spouses will want to welcome other leaders and their spouses into one another's homes. For only when we invite one another into our homes can we begin to know one another. On home ground pretence becomes more difficult. Furthermore, not only does the leadership team benefit from mutual friendships; the church as a whole also benefits when leaders enjoy friendship together. For friendships amongst leaders often have a 'trickle-down' effect: they encourage the development of friendships amongst the membership in general.

Praying for one another

Praying for one another is a duty every Christian owes to one another (see James 5.16). It is good too for leaders to pray for one another, and in this way help bear one another's burdens (Galatians 6.2). For leadership can be tough—and life can be tough too! Hopefully such prayer for one another is not viewed as a duty, but rather as a natural expression of concern for one another. For to pray for one another is just another way of loving one another (see Matthew 5.44).

THE ART OF LEADERSHIP

'I exhort the elders among you to tend the flock of God that is in your charge, exercising the oversight, not under compulsion, but willingly, as God would have you do it—not for sordid gain but eagerly. Do not lord it over those in your charge, but be examples to the flock.'

I Peter 5.1b–3

Let the leaders lead!

Leadership is a key priority in today's churches. Leaders do the Lord and his church a disservice if they do not exercise their gifts and offer leadership. The fact that there have been those who have abused their position and have 'lorded it over those in their charge' is no argument against leadership *per se*. Rightly understood, leadership does not stand in opposition to service. It is an expression of service. Churches are the poorer where leaders fail to lead.

As research in recent years has clearly indicated, the degree to which churches grow and develop and make any kind of impact on our increasingly pagan world, is largely dependent on the kind of leadership that is exercised in them.

It has been said that 'churches need more leaders, not more members'. At first sight such a statement may appear to be an exaggeration. And yet there is truth in it. For once we have the right leaders, membership problems will begin to be solved—for with the right leadership effective strategies for mission can be implemented and hopefully people will be won for Christ and his church. True, at the end of the day we are dependent upon the Holy Spirit—and yet part of the art of leadership is setting the sails to catch the wind of the Spirit.

Clearly pastors have a key role to play in exercising leadership. But so too do deacons and elders. As we have already seen, leadership in the New Testament was always corporate. There are limits to what one person can achieve on their own. Pastors need to work with a leadership team.

Defining leadership

But what precisely is leadership? The New Testament points to many qualities needed within leadership, but does not develop a model as such. However, one helpful model of leadership developed by John Adair has defined the good leader as one who 'works as a senior partner with other members to achieve the task, build the team, and meet individual needs'. Translated into language associated with the Christian church 'the other members' with whom the pastor as 'senior partner' works are the leaders of the church. Together the leaders face these three challenges.

1 Achieving the task

Within a Christian frame of reference, the task is the mission of the church. This mission might be interpreted in large general terms relating to the overall implementation of the Great Commission. On the other hand, the mission might be interpreted in more specific terms, relating to the particular mission of a local church in a given area at a given time.

Needless to say, before the task may be achieved, it must first be defined. Such a defining of the task involves the leaders putting before the church a vision of what God is calling his people to be and do. Many churches find it helpful in this respect to develop a mission statement for the church's life together: e.g. on the basis of the Great Commission as found in Matthew 28.18–20 and John 20.21 a church might state, 'Our mission is to go Christ's way and make disciples'. However, mission statements by themselves are of limited value. Aims and objectives need to be developed, along with appropriate strategies. This is the task of leadership. Of course, these aims and objectives and strategies will need to be accepted and owned by the church meeting—but the task of leadership is enabling the church meeting to grasp the vision.

2 Building the team

Within a Christian frame of reference the church is the team. What's more, the church is a team with a task. Every-member-ministry is suddenly given direction. There is a common goal to which all can work. The task of leaders within the church is continually to seek to weld the team together by giving it a sense of common purpose and direction. When relationship difficulties arise, then leaders must be prepared to deal with such difficulties. For healing and harmony to prevail, this may involve confronting those who need to be confronted. At other times leaders may need to act as peace-brokers and go-betweens. 'Teamsmanship'—the art of becoming a team-player—must constantly be worked at. Leaders have a particular responsibility to 'make every effort to maintain the unity of the Spirit in the bond of peace' (Ephesians 4.3).

3 Meeting the needs of individuals

If members of the team are to work effectively as they seek to achieve the task, then their individual needs have to be met. What are these needs? It seems to me that they are five-fold: church members need to be led in worship, to be taught, to receive pastoral care, to experience fellowship and to find avenues of service. The task of leaders is to ensure that all these needs are met. It is as these basic needs are met that members are 'equipped … for the work of ministry' (Ephesians 4.11).

Mastering change

If the mission of the church is to be fulfilled, then change will have to be introduced. No church can afford to stand still. We live in a rapidly changing world, and so 'constant change is here to stay' as much in the church as in the world. We can no longer rely upon yesterday's successes—we must, for instance, find new ways of doing evangelism and being church.

In so far as the Gospel is all about being a 'new creation' (2 Corinthians 5.17) one might well think that Christians would take to change as ducks to water. Sadly this is not always the case. Churches can be as resistant to change as any other institution. For leaders to effectively master change, they must be 'as wise as serpents' (Matthew 10.16) and understand two things in particular.

1 Change involves time

If major change is proposed, then leaders need to give the church sufficient time to think the issue through. One church meeting is often insufficient. Some major changes may well take several months to effect. Indeed, some changes are best brought about on an experimental basis: i.e. a church agrees to allow change to take place in a particular area of its life on the understanding that six months down the track the whole issue is reviewed. If the experiment proves a success, then the church simply confirms the wisdom of the original decision!

2 Change involves a process

If leaders are to take the church as a whole with them, they must pay careful attention to the various rates of adoption as also to the various categories of adopters. These rates and categories have been classified by E. M. Rogers and F. F. Shoemaker (*The Communication Of Innovations*, Collier Macmillan, New York, 1971) as follows:

1   Some 2.5% of the church are *Innovators*, who are enthusiastic about change and promote its introduction to others.

2   A further 13.5% are *Early Adopters*, who are quick to accept the change, and are then happy to promote its introduction.

3   A further 34% form the *Early Majority*. Many initially had reservations, but have now been persuaded and now persuade others.

4   A further 34%, the *Late Majority*, were initially resistant to the change, but have been gradually won over.

5   The final 16% are the *Laggards* who now accept the change grudgingly. The dissidents remain in this group even after the change has become tradition!

Obviously there is a good deal of generalisation here. In small churches, for instance, one or other of these categories may be absent or disproportionately represented. Furthermore, the composition of these groups may vary according to the type of change being considered. And yet it is important for leaders to deal with the underlying dynamics relating to the process of change. If a church is not to be split unnecessarily leaders need to ensure that decisions are not taken at church meeting until the 'Late Majority' has come on board. This does not guarantee unanimity—there will always be some die-hard 'Laggards'. However, without the 'Late Majority' a church risks literally being split in two. Clearly there is no Scriptural foundation to such an analysis. However, not to pay attention to such insights is to run the risk of being what Paul describes as 'children in your thinking' (1 Corinthians 14.20).

Managing conflict

The management of change involves managing conflict. It is no exaggeration to say that where two or three are gathered in Jesus' name, then there is almost bound to be some conflict at one time or another. Certainly, this was the experience of the New Testament churches. The 'conflicts and disputes' (James 4.1) of which James speaks can be mirrored in all the Pauline churches too. Leaders need to be realistic in their understanding of human nature.

Realism, however, does not mean that we accept human nature as it is. Leaders need to ensure, for instance, that in the church meeting 'the truth is spoken in love' (Ephesians 4.15). This means, for instance, that leaders need to ensure that conflict is depersonalised—that issues and not personalities are discussed. The church meeting needs to know that it is OK to disagree and to express alternative points of views; but it is not OK to disagree in anger or with hostility. The church also needs to be helped to understand that what is at issue in a church meeting is not winning a point, but discovering the will of God. If the will of God is to be discovered, then everybody needs to listen to one another. It is significant that Paul in his lists of spiritual gifts links the gift of 'discernment' with the gift of 'prophecy' (1 Corinthians 12.8). Every contribution in a church meeting has to be weighed—or as John puts it, if we are not to be led astray by 'false prophets' we need to 'test the spirits to see whether they are from God' (1 John 4.1). One of the key tasks of Christian leadership is ensuring that differences of opinion are handled in a truly Christian manner.

The fact is that differences of opinion are not always to be feared. Often they are to be welcomed. A church without any disagreements may well be a church where nothing is happening. Churches without some form of low-level conflict are probably churches where the leaders are not doing their job in seeking to lead out the people of God in adventurous mission. Differences of opinion can be a sign of life.

Not all conflict will necessarily surface within the church meeting. Sometimes, for instance, a conflict may involve two church members; alternatively a conflict of interest may develop between two organisations wanting to use the church premises on the same day. On such occasions church leaders should be prepared to get involved and help the individuals or organisations concerned to resolve their differences. Disunity dishonours Christ.

THE CHALLENGE OF
PASTORAL CARE

'Leaders ... are keeping watch over your souls and will give an account. Let them do this with joy.'
Hebrews 13.17

In the first place pastoral care is the responsibility of every member. Paul, for instance, spoke of the members having 'the same care for one another' (1 Corinthians 12.25). He urged the Galatians to 'bear each other's burdens' which in turn involved caring for those straying from the faith (Galatians 6.1–2). Paul expected the Thessalonians to share in every aspect of pastoral care: 'admonish the idlers, encourage the fainthearted, help the weak' (1 Thessalonians 5.14). Similarly the Colossians were to 'teach and admonish one another in all wisdom' (Colossians 3.16).

However, pastoral care is also a special responsibility of leaders. In the words of Paul to the Ephesian elders at Miletus, they are to 'keep watch ... over all the flock, of which the Holy Spirit has made you overseers, to shepherd the church of God that he obtained with the blood of his own Son' (Acts 20.28). In practical terms this involves:

Knowing everybody

Just as the good shepherd knows all his sheep by name (John 10.3), so too should those who exercise care in the name of the good shepherd. In smaller churches this may be no problem; in larger churches where visitors may often be present this may pose quite a challenge. Unlike their American cousins, British people are sometimes 'bad' at names—actually, it is not that Americans are cleverer than us, rather because in their culture it is bad form not to know a person's name, Americans tend to make a much greater effort. Such effort should also characterise leaders in a British Baptist church.

To help leaders—as indeed everybody—to get to know people, it is useful to produce a church handbook in which are listed not only the names, addresses, and telephone numbers of members, but also the names of friends and of non-Christian spouses (we should be able to pray for them by name, even if they do not attend church). Members can always be distinguished from friends by the printing of a small asterisk by their name! In addition, the names of children—not least those who have been brought for a service of dedication—should be included in the handbook. In larger churches the names will no doubt be listed in alphabetical order of surname—however, small churches might consider listing the names in alphabetical order of Christian names—this practise certainly encourages relationships to be on first name terms. However it is

24

done, with such a handbook, updated on a yearly basis, the learning of names should be made much easier.

Welcoming visitors

Like the Good Shepherd who is concerned for the sheep who do not belong to his fold (John 10.16), leaders too will want to be outward looking. Rightly understood, pastoral care can never be exclusive. Precisely how such care is directed toward visitors will vary from church to church. In some churches one of the responsibilities of leaders is to form a 'door duty' welcome rota—in other churches this welcome rota is shared with other members too. Needless to say, a formal handshake coupled with a few words of greeting does not necessarily equate with a welcome. While it is true that some visitors may wish to remain anonymous, most people appreciate the offer of friendship. Such an offer may be expressed in inviting the visitor(s) back to lunch, or if it's an evening service, back home for a coffee. Clearly the exercise of hospitality is not the exclusive preserve of leaders, but Paul's instructions to Timothy suggest that leaders should set an example in this area (1 Timothy 3.2).

Interviewing for membership

In many Baptist churches leaders will often be involved—along with others—in visiting applicants for membership. On these occasions the conversation will in part centre around the responsibilities of church membership, and no doubt the opportunity will be taken to discern the gifts and skills the prospective new members have to offer. However, such visiting can also be a form of pastoral care, for there is also the opportunity to talk sensitively about where the potential members are in their Christian pilgrimage and to offer them appropriate encouragement and help. Hopefully that initial conversation will then prove the basis for many subsequent meaningful conversations. Indeed, in some churches the visitors for church membership are given responsibility for keeping a watchful eye on those they have visited for a period of say, twelve months.

Exercising church discipline

Church discipline is also a form of pastoral care. Sadly in some churches church discipline has almost been equated with the last rites—when offending church members are deemed to be almost beyond hope, because in one way or another they have flagrantly overstepped the mark (often through some kind of sexual misdemeanour) their names are brought to the leaders and then to the church meeting with a view to removal from the church roll. Church discipline, however, need to begin at a much earlier stage—while there is still hope. The aim of church discipline is to bring a person back to the Lord, not to send them packing (see Galatians 6.1). Furthermore, church discipline needs to be concerned for every aspect of the Christian life: constant gossip and criticism is as much in need of being dealt with as, for example, sins of a sexual nature. Likewise when a church meeting has been spoilt by ill-temper or by unloving remarks of one kind or another, the leaders have a responsibility for making it clear that such behaviour is unacceptable. Church discipline may involve private pastoral visits to individuals who are judged to be at fault. It may also lead to having to make a public statement at the church meeting (see Matthew 18.15–20). Leaders have a responsibility in safeguarding the spiritual health of the church.

Revising the church roll

Another form of pastoral care is the annual revision of the church roll. It is difficult to encourage people to take their membership responsibilities seriously, when there are members who have not attended the church for several years. Because roll revision can be a sensitive issue, it is helpful if before any revision is undertaken the church as a whole is clear as to what is the precise basis of the revision. For example: 'Once members have left the area for more than a period of twelve months, their membership will lapse. When members living in the area do not attend church at all in a twelve-month period, they will be visited, and unless there is some good reason (e.g. ill health or old age) their membership will lapse. However, their names will be retained in the church handbook in the category of friends for a further period of two years'. Hopefully the steps taken to prune the roll will result in many instances not in deletion of a name, but in restoration to fellowship. Roll revision is painful, and yet—in the words of Jesus' parable of the vine—a branch is pruned 'to make it bear more fruit' (John 15.2).

Visiting the fellowship

Pastoral visiting is as much the responsibility of the leaders of the church as that of the pastor. In this respect Acts 6 is particularly instructive: there seven men were appointed to care for the widows in the church, so that the apostles were freed for their ministry of the word and of prayer. The principle is clear: those who have been appointed to minister God's Word to his people cannot be responsible for caring for all those in their care—they need others to share with them that responsibility and in this way free them up for the particular tasks to which God has called them. Clearly where there is a 'crisis'—and in many families births and marriages are as much 'crises' as deaths, in the sense that in their own way they cause the people involved to be often asking major questions of life—pastors will want to be involved. Routine pastoral visiting, however, should be very much the brief of other members—and not least leaders—of the fellowship.

Encouraging growth

Pastoral care has a much broader base than simply helping people in one kind of trouble or another. Rightly understood, pastoral care includes helping, encouraging and enabling people to grow and develop in the Christian faith.

In the words of the Apostle Paul, it is about the presentation of 'everyone perfect in Christ' (Colossians 1.28,29). Sometimes this involves helping members who are stuck in their walk with their Lord, to get going and growing again. At other times it may involve enabling members to deal with past hurts and gain the courage to forgive and move on. If pastoral care is to have any depth, then it needs to go beyond passing the time of day with people. In a gentle and sensitive fashion, leaders need to be able to talk with others about their spiritual lives: where they have been, where they are now, and where by God's grace they would like to go.

Developing a system of pastoral care

Precisely how that pastoral responsibility is shared will vary from church to church. In some churches every leader is viewed as a 'pastoral' leader. The list of the church's members and friends is then split amongst the leaders, each of whom is then responsible for caring for those in their charge. Opportunities are then given at every leaders' meeting for pastoral news and concerns to be shared. There are, however, some disadvantages to this system: in the first place, it assumes that every leader is pastorally gifted, whereas in fact most leadership teams reflect a mixture of gifts; in the second place, it assumes that every leader has time to care, whereas in fact some leaders may just be too busy because of responsibilities at work or indeed in the church. The upshot is that with such a system, pastoral care tends to be patchy.

In other churches responsibility for day-to-day pastoral care is given to those leaders who have the gifts and the time. Together they can form a 'pastoral team'. Clearly there can be many variations on this system. In some churches the pastoral team is expanded to include members who are not on the leadership team to help in the task of pastoral care. In larger churches the pastoral team may delegate some of its tasks to 'care group leaders' of one kind or another. There is no one particular pattern which Baptist churches should follow. The underlying principle is that pastoral care is shared in a way so that care is effectively given to all God's people.

PASTORS ALSO NEED LOOKING AFTER

'God has so arranged the body … that there may be no dissension within the body, but the members may have the same care for one another.'

I Corinthians 12.24,25

In many churches the above verses have been rewritten: 'God has so arranged the body … that the pastors may have the care of the body', with the result that nobody within the church takes responsibility for caring for the pastor. But pastors—and their families—are in as much need of pastoral care as anybody else. For pastors and their families are human too—like everybody else they are subject to all the stresses and strains of modern life. Furthermore, in a way which is not always true of others, they are particularly subject to all the strains and stresses of church life. What's more, the Baptist Union through its Regional Ministers and the Department of Ministry can offer only limited support. The key carers of pastors are the churches whom they serve.

As Paul in 1 Corinthians 12 implies, in one sense the whole church has a responsibility for its pastor. And as many pastors can in fact testify, many members do a wonderful job of caring, not least by constantly encouraging them and praying regularly for them.

However, in so far as the leaders are responsible for the pastoral oversight of the church, they have a particular responsibility for their pastors and their families. Just as once a year the leaders have to review the pastor's stipend, so at least once a year the general well-being of the pastor—and family where appropriate—should also be an agenda item. But such pastoral care should, of course, be more than an agenda item. Pastoral care should be ongoing. In particular leaders can care for their pastor in the following ways.

Praying for the pastor

Leaders, like other members, are able to pray daily for their pastor. As the Apostle Paul reminds us, as Christians we are engaged in a spiritual battle (Ephesians 6.12)—and often the pastor is at the sharp end of the conflict. Like Aaron and Hur supporting Moses in prayer (Exodus 17.12), leaders should want to support their pastor. What's more, prayer is needed not simply for the ongoing tasks of ministry, but also for the pastor's personal life. If the Devil can cause trouble to the pastor and the pastor's family, then the whole church is in trouble. On Sundays leaders also have a special opportunity to pray with—and for—their pastor before each service. This prayer-time before the service can have a significant role in 'warming up' the pastor before the service starts. It's helpful therefore for as many leaders as possible to be present—and what's more to be present in good time!

Encouraging the pastor

All of us need affirmation and encouragement (1 Thessalonians 5.11)—and this is equally true of pastors. Pastors have their ups and downs. Leaders in particular should look for ways to give encouragement. If God has spoken through a sermon, then mention it. When things have gone well, express appreciation. Even when things have not gone so well, seek to discern the positives among the negatives!

Defending the pastor

When difficulties arise, as inevitably they do (see, for instance, 3 John 9.10), leaders should always be ready to defend their pastor against unfair criticism. In principle, pastors are Christ's gift to his church (Ephesians 4.12) and should be respected as such. Even where the criticism is fair, in the first place leaders should speak privately to the pastor, face to face, rather than join in the public criticism.

It is often said that the church secretary is the person who represents the pastor to the church and the church to the pastor. Yet sometimes there is a conflict of interests as far as the church secretary is concerned. This can be especially true where difficulties arise which are of the pastor's own making. In such a situation it can be helpful for the leaders to ensure that somebody is able to speak on the pastor's behalf and represent the concerns of the pastor.

If serious difficulties are threatened, there is much to be said for bringing in from outside the church a respected Christian leader: e.g. an Association representative or a Regional Minister.

Providing opportunities for study

This is one sure way of guaranteeing freshness and depth in the pastor's ministry! Although patterns of work have become increasingly flexible, there is much to be said for encouraging pastors to spend every morning in study and preparation. For this to happen, these study periods should be respected and not trespassed on, except in emergencies. Pastors need to be encouraged to take the recommended study-leave of a week a year, and a three month sabbatical every seven years after ordination. Needless to say, leaders need to ensure that the church makes appropriate provision for the cost of study. Books and journals are important (see 2 Timothy 4.13), but they can be expensive, as also conferences. At the end of the day, however, the church never loses out on such investment!

Providing office facilities

In the first place, this may mean ensuring that there is an office in the church from which the pastor can work. Such an arrangement can be advantageous to the church, since it can encourage the pastor to be more disciplined. Many pastors also find it a great advantage to have an office at church, so that home can become home. Whatever, wherever the pastor works, the appropriate tools need to be available. In today's terms this means that pastors should have access to church computers (with broadband internet connection!), printers, and photocopiers—it is not fair for pastors to have to buy their own office equipment. Secretarial assistance—even if it be limited—is also essential, if the pastor is not to get bogged down in administrative tasks. All this is part of the leaders' responsibility to free the pastor for the ministry of the word and of prayer (Acts 6.2).

Ensuring adequate time off

Ultimately nobody benefits—not even the church—if the pastor works morning, noon and night. Effective pastors are disciplined pastors, and this affects leisure as well as work. At the very least this means that pastors observe the principle of the sabbath and have one formal day off in the week, which nobody may be allowed to disturb. Leaders need to ensure that everybody in the church knows and respects that particular day. The pastor's day off, which can vary from week to week, can usefully be publicised in the church magazine or weekly newssheet. In addition, pastors should be encouraged to take time off at other periods in the week too. Almost no one else in the church works six days a week. Likewise leaders need to ensure that their pastor takes the full holiday allowance—pastors can only fulfil their ministry effectively if they are fresh in the Lord's service.

Paying a fair stipend

'The labourer deserves to be paid' (Luke 10.7) said Jesus. Indeed, Paul told Timothy that those who 'rule well be considered worthy of double honour, especially those who labour in preaching and teaching' (1 Timothy 5.17): as the GNB with its translation of 'double pay' makes clear, such 'honour' has financial implications! Clearly a pastor's stipend will be dependent upon what a church can actually afford to pay—some churches, for instance, will be receiving help from Baptist Union Home Mission. Nonetheless it is only right that leaders ensure their pastor is fairly treated.

Leaders also need to ensure that their pastor's stipend is dealt with in a sensitive and tactful manner. It is not helpful if every year there is a discussion in the church meeting of how much the pastor is worth. For those churches not in receipt of Home Mission funding, there is much to be said for establishing some principle by which the minister's stipend is worked out. The stipend may, for instance, be based on the Home Mission stipend, or on a percentage increase above the Home Mission stipend; alternatively the stipend may relate to an agreed basket of salaries in the secular world. Some imagination is required in this area.

Providing comfortable housing (or an adequate housing allowance)

Related to the stipend is the issue of housing. An increasing number of pastors now own their own homes—in such instances a fair housing allowance needs to be paid in addition to the stipend. However, where pastors are living in a church manse, then leaders need to ensure that the manse is of a sufficient size for the pastor's needs. Furthermore, they need to ensure that the church properly looks after the manse. A fabric inspection of the manse should be carried out on an annual basis, and a report, agreed by pastor and fabric steward, should be brought to the leaders' meeting. Where the pastor is married, then the pastor's spouse should also be a party to the agreed report!

Setting up a system for an annual review of performance and development

Annual reviews—sometimes known as appraisals—give an opportunity for leaders to affirm their pastor and to say 'well done', to review previously set objectives and set future goals, to provide a safe environment for discussing problems and, where necessary, to express dissatisfaction, and to identify needs for further training and development. Rightly understood, review is a positive process.

In many ways review is more helpful to ministers than almost any other group of workers. For ministry is by and large a lonely profession. Ministers for the most part work on their own. The annual review can break down some of the isolationism and in doing so prove extremely supportive.

There is no one way in which such ministerial reviews should be conducted. It is really down to each church to develop their own model. However, experience has shown that it is helpful to bring in an outside facilitator—preferably an experienced minister—who can help the leaders work through the process, and who can also stand with the pastor in what may at first sight appear to be a threatening process.

HANDLING PASTORAL TRANSITIONS

So far in this guide we have been assuming that, along with the leaders, there is always a pastor in place. Although some churches for financial reasons may not be in a position to employ a pastor, a pastor-led church is the norm for Baptists. However, inevitably the time comes when the pastor moves on, and at such a point a good deal more work falls upon the shoulders of the leaders. From now on they have all the responsibility for the church's ministry and mission. This can be a heavy responsibility.

Farewelling the pastor

On the basis of Baptist Union guidelines, it is customary for ministers to give their church at least three months' notice of their intention to leave the pastorate. Three months' notice may sound generous, but in a church context those months speed by. From the ministers' point of view, although they may continue to work out their notice in a diligent fashion, inevitably their ministry changes gear. No longer is their focus on the future. They are simply engaged in the day-to-day business of pastoral ministry. There is also a subtle shift as far as their members are concerned. They too are now aware of the temporary nature of the ministry. Already the pastor is no longer the leader of the church—the mantle has now fallen on the leadership team.

One of the tasks of leadership at this stage is to ensure that the ministry ends on a positive note. This is all the more true if there have been differences in the church which have perhaps led to the decision of the minister to move on. The past cannot be undone. However, in a Christian context it should always be possible for the parties to leave at peace with one another (see Romans 12.17,18).

It is good to be able to mark the minister's last weekend at the church in a festive way. Many churches, for instance, like to put on some social occasion at which former members are invited to return and give thanks for the past ministry. Along with words of thanks, tangible expressions of gratitude are normally given—a bouquet of flowers, a generous cheque, and gifts for the children where appropriate. It's right and proper to be generous to those who have been our teachers (Galatians 6.6).

Appointing a 'chair'

In the absence of a minister, the first step a leadership team needs to take is to appoint a 'chair' for its meetings. In many cases the church secretary is the natural person to assume this responsibility. However, in some churches there may be another senior deacon who may be deemed to be more suitably gifted for this task (see 1 Corinthians 12.8).

There are times when it may be good to bring in an 'outsider' to help chair the meetings of the leadership team or the church meeting. The search for a new minister can prove quite demanding, not least perhaps when there are varying opinions held within the church as to the kind of pastor the church needs. In such a context it can often be helpful to appoint an outside 'moderator' who can act as an impartial chair when the leadership team or the church meets to consider the future pastorate. It helps too when the moderator is a Baptist minister with experience of settlement procedures within Baptist churches. However gifted a leadership team may be, it still can benefit from wise advice (see Proverbs 12.15; 13.10).

Beginning the search for a new pastor

Although it is not normally a good idea to bring any name to the church meeting before the previous pastor has left—apart from anything else the church needs time to grieve its loss—there is no reason why the search should not begin as soon as notice has been given. In many churches the leadership team as a whole forms the 'search committee'. In some churches, however, a small search committee is set up, often as a sub-committee of the leadership team, with perhaps one or two co-opted members.

As part of the search, a church 'profile' needs to be drawn up, which provides a description not only of the present activities of the church but also of possible future opportunities for mission and ministry (see 1 Corinthians 16.9). The drawing up of the church profile can be quite a creative exercise.

At an early stage it is helpful to invite a Regional Minister to come and meet with the search committee. Although Regional Ministers in no way control ministerial movements, they can be helpful facilitators of such movements. At the same time it is good for individual church members to feel free to suggest names of possible future ministers. Experience shows, however, that it is normally wise to restrict candidates to men and women whose names are on the Baptist Union's list of accredited ministers.

The Regional Ministers themselves issue some very helpful guidelines on seeking a new minister. Those guidelines should be carefully studied. The fact is that church meetings find it easiest to consider one person at a time. Confusion otherwise tends to reign.

Maintaining the ministry

As churches who are never able to afford ministers know only too well, maintaining the ministry of the church in the absence of a full-time leader is a demanding task. Preachers have to be found, pastoral care has to be exercised, and mission to the world has to go on. Needless to say, such responsibilities have to be delegated. One member of the leadership team, for instance, may have to be responsible for preachers, another for pastoral care, and another for mission.

On the positive side, the experience of many churches is that a period without a minister can prove to be a very fruitful period. It is often then that churches discover new gifts in their midst, and what's more the period without formal ministry provides an opportunity for those gifts to be used and developed (Romans 12.5–8).

Some churches may be able to follow the American custom of appointing an 'interim minister'. Interim ministers by definition are not permanent ministers. Often retired ministers or ministers not in the employment of a local church, their chief responsibilities are the Sunday preaching and a certain amount of limited pastoral care. Interim ministers can provide a useful service not just in maintaining the ministry, but also in paving the way for a new minister, particularly if there have been some unresolved pastoral problems linked with the previous pastorate.

Calling a new pastor

The mechanics of calling a new pastor are all helpfully dealt with in guidelines produced by the Baptist Union in their booklet *Facing a Pastoral Vacancy*. Traditionally for Baptists everything hinges on the Sunday when the prospective minister preaches 'with a view'. Certainly the way in which worship is led and the Word is expounded speak volumes about a person and are key to any ministry. However, it is important for the leadership team to use its imagination in providing other opportunities for members of the church to meet with the prospective minister.

Suffice it to say, the calling of a new pastor is one of the most important decisions a church can ever make. It is therefore important that as many members as possible are present at the subsequent church meeting. If this means arranging the church meeting for a Sunday afternoon, rather than its normal mid-week slot, so be it.

Hopefully at the end of the process the church can say of its decision that 'it has seemed good to the Holy Spirit and to us' (Acts 15.28).

Welcoming the new pastor

The 'induction' service is the occasion when the new minister is formally welcomed and recognised as the church's new pastor. Traditionally such services have been held on a Saturday, when representatives from other churches can be present—not least perhaps the members of the new minister's previous church. However, today there is much to be said for considering holding the induction on a Sunday, when almost certainly a higher proportion of the church's members and friends will be present. True, this may mean that representatives of other churches may have to miss their own service—but so what? The chief purpose of the induction is for the local church to express its welcome. Again, the leadership team needs to be imaginative in its thinking. Make the day a day to remember—with helium-filled balloons for all the children and scrumptious food for all. Let the people of God party!

OPPORTUNITIES FOR FURTHER MINISTRY ABOUND

'Now there are varieties of gifts … varieties of services … and varieties of activities.'
                                                                    1 Corinthians 12.4–6

The task of leadership is multi-faceted. What is more, not every leader is expected to be a carbon copy of another—for God gifts leaders in different ways for differing forms of Christian service. Nonetheless, there are certain tasks which are generally common to all members of the leadership team

Serving at the Lord's Table

In Baptist churches it is the custom for leaders to help in the serving of the bread and wine. The historical roots of this custom probably go back to a time when Nonconformists wished to emphasise the priesthood of all believers (see 1 Peter 2.5,9)—they had no need of a priest to give them bread and wine! There is no Biblical ground for reserving this task for leaders alone—indeed in some churches, past leaders are also invited from time to time to share in this service. However, the theological symbolism of leaders serving those in their care is a telling one and reflects the servant nature of leadership (see Luke 22.26).

In many ways the serving of bread and wine is an undemanding task—often the most demanding aspect is simply remembering who is on the rota for that particular service! However, there is one aspect which can be overlooked. Inevitably, as leaders serve the bread and wine, they will notice that on occasions there are members who allow the plate or cup to pass them by. On such occasions there is much to be said for a sensitive enquiry after the service: for example, 'I happened to notice that this morning you did not choose to take communion. Are things OK? I just wondered whether there is any way in which I could be of help to you'.

Praying at the Lord's Table

In many Baptist churches it is not the pastor, but rather one of the other leaders who gives thanks for the bread and wine. Again the historical roots of this custom probably lie in a Nonconformist desire to emphasise that they need no priest to consecrate the elements. In other Christian traditions the prayer of thanksgiving is reserved for the priest to say and is regarded as the church's central prayer. In the light of all this it becomes clear that it is no small privilege and responsibility to take this prayer. It is therefore wise for leaders to come prepared. Some find it helpful as part of their preparation to find out beforehand the theme of the pastor's sermon so that their prayer can neatly dovetail. Incidentally, although for Baptists extempore prayer is the order of the day in the home and in prayer meetings, there is much to be said for writing out the communion prayer so that well-worn phrases and pious cliches are avoided. The Spirit's inspiration is not limited to the spontaneous!

It is important to note the primary purpose of the prayer: it is a prayer of 'thanksgiving' (1 Corinthians 11.24). It is therefore normally inappropriate to include a prayer of confession—almost certainly the congregation has been led in such a prayer at the beginning of the service. Nor is it appropriate to bring before God the needs of the fellowship—almost certainly there is a 'pastoral' prayer yet to come. No, the prayer needs to be one of praise and thanksgiving for the Lord Jesus.

If a guide is required, then take a look at the second eucharistic prayer in the Anglican *Alternative Service Book*. It is a wonderful credal prayer of thanksgiving:

It is indeed right,
It is our duty and our joy,
at all times and in all places
to give you thanks and praise,
holy Father, heavenly King,
almighty and eternal God,
through Jesus Christ your only Son our Lord.

For he is your living Word;
through him you have created all things from the beginning,
and formed us in your own image.

Through him you have freed us from the slavery of sin,
giving him to be born as man and to die upon the cross;
you raised him from the dead
and exalted him to your right hand on high.

Through him you have sent upon us
your holy and life-giving Spirit,
and made us a people for your own possession.

Therefore with angels and archangels
and with all the company of heaven,
we proclaim your great and glorious name …

Praying for baptismal candidates

Many churches have revived the old Baptist practice of baptism being followed by prayer with laying-on of hands. This custom, of course, is not specifically Baptist, but rather goes back to Scripture (see Acts 8.17; 19.6; Hebrews 6.2).

Very often leaders are involved in praying for the baptismal candidates. In the light of such passages as Matthew 3.16,17 and Acts 1.8, it is important to note that the purpose of such prayer is to invoke the Spirit to come and fill the candidates with fresh power for service. As the candidates have been baptised in water, so a fresh baptism of the Spirit is requested. The candidates have already received the Spirit, but now they desire yet more of him. Some churches link this practice with the giving of a 'text' to the candidates (written on the baptismal certificate). If this is done, then before prayer is made the 'text' can be publicly given and then woven into the following prayer.

Leading in worship and teaching

Then there are other tasks, particularly relating to worship and teaching, which will be undertaken by leaders according to their gifting. For example, some may well be in involved in leading worship; others in preaching; yet others in leading small groups of one kind or another. Increasingly one-person ministry is becoming a thing of the past in Baptist churches; opportunities for ministry abound.

Serving as church officers

Other leadership tasks relate to office. Traditionally in a Baptist church there are two key church officers: the church secretary and the church treasurer. These two officers, together with the pastor, normally form the church 'executive'.

1   The church secretary

The church secretary is appointed by the church as its senior officer and serves both the leadership team and the church meeting. The responsibilities of a church secretary include maintaining a broad overview of the life of the church, using opportunities to present the vision and the aims of the church, troubleshooting whenever necessary, listening to the concerns of church members, consulting regularly with the pastor, together with the pastor drawing up the agenda of the leadership team meeting and of the church meeting, keeping abreast of Baptist Union issues, keeping abreast of legislation which affects the church (e.g. data protection, health and safety), and corresponding with outside organisations and persons on behalf of the church on official matters.

2   The church treasurer

The church treasurer's responsibilities can be divided into two: first of all marrying together vision and financial resources by engendering enthusiasm for giving, developing innovative ways of increasing income, and preparing the budget and the accounts; secondly controlling the church's expenditure by overseeing all aspects of the church's insurances, ensuring that all cash and other receipts are properly controlled and recorded, ensuring the maintenance of all necessary book keeping records, overseeing the Gift Aided giving, dealing with all aspects of paying ministerial stipends, and allocating money to 'outside' causes as agreed by the church meeting.

In small churches there may be a shortage of the ideal skills noted above. For example, the pastor, if there is one, may find that some tasks of a church secretary may have to be undertaken by him/her.

Similarly the ideal church treasurer may not be available. Even basic competences required when a pastor has to be paid may be absent. In such a case, rather than muddle through, urgent search will need to be made outside the leadership—or maybe even the membership—so that financial matters are ordered with due care. Meanwhile the leaders should consider who amongst them or the members might receive the necessary training for the bare minimum of the work of a treasurer.

Encouraging the mission and ministry of the church

Important as the tasks of church secretary and church treasurer are, there are other significant offices in the life of the church. Indeed, if a leadership team simply focuses on administration and finance, it very easily gets into the maintenance mode. But for a church to be true to its Lord, mission and ministry are also required.

At the very least, for instance, one leader needs to be given responsibility for mission, and another responsibility for nurture and development.

In a slightly bigger church the leadership team might be able to break down these tasks in a way that makes them even more specific: for instance, one leader might be responsible for social action, another for evangelism, another for nurture, and yet another for training and development.

In a large church, small teams—each perhaps led by a member of the overall leadership team—may be drawn together for specific tasks, which would cover defined areas of the church's mission and ministry. Where this happens the mandate of the team members should not be to do all the work themselves, but rather to empower and encourage others in the church to get behind whatever may be their particular project. Their membership needs to be approved by and accountable to the church meeting, and their activities should be monitored by the leadership team. Ideally every aspect of church life should come under the purview of the teams. This would mean, for instance, that the leaders of all church organisations and activities would be accountable to the church meeting through the task-oriented teams, which would in turn be responsible for both providing support and ensuring that the work of all church organisations and activities is in line with the church's overall strategy. From the perspective of a small church, where there is often a shortage of people with essential skills, the organisation of a large church may seem incredibly complicated. Yet the underlying principle is simple: task-oriented teams in larger churches represent the extension of the principle that those with gifts of leadership should be empowered to serve God in and through his church. It is a way of giving expression to 'the leadership of some'. In addition, of course, these teams also afford opportunities for other members to exercise and develop their own gifts.

Needless to say, there is no one pattern for any church to follow. It is up to each church to develop a model of mission and ministry which is appropriate to them and which best enables the church to fulfil the Great Commission.

Ordering Leaders' Meetings

'All things should be done decently and in order.'

1 Corinthians 14.40

If leaders' meetings had been a matter of contention in the life of the New Testament churches, we might have had some guidance from one or other apostle as to how they should be run. As it is, the New Testament is silent on this issue. Nonetheless, Paul's rubric for worship (1 Corinthians 14.40) is surely also applicable to the way in which we conduct our church business. The fact that we come together to seek God's guidance does not make the need for order any less necessary: the Spirit works within (as also outside) structures!

From this the question then arises: how might we most effectively order our meetings today? What are the most helpful structures through which leaders can seek the mind of Christ with regard to the life of their church?

Meeting monthly

How frequently should leaders meet? Clearly there is no hard-and-fast rule. Most leaders conduct their business on a monthly basis, although there are churches where their leaders meet on a fortnightly, or even a weekly basis. However, unless a church is going through a period of crisis there seems no good reason why leaders cannot restrict their business to a monthly meeting. The fact is that for most deacons life is incredibly pressurised. Responsibilities at work or in the church can be enormous. It makes good sense to restrict regular leaders' meetings to once a month, for we owe it to God to be good stewards of our time (Ephesians 5.16). Clearly such a principle does not rule out 'specials' from time to time.

Agreeing a venue

The early church never faced the issue of whether to meet at church or in a home—they only had homes! The dynamics of meeting around a formal 'board' table at church are very different from sitting on comfortable chairs in one another's homes. The latter is certainly more relaxing—on the other hand, there is no virtue in being so relaxed in the Lord's business that the meetings take twice as long to achieve half the business!

Prioritising the agenda

An agenda reflects the spiritual priorities of a church. In too many churches the top three items on the agenda of a leaders' meeting are: (i) finance;

(ii) fabric; (iii) correspondence. Such agendas are surely the death-knell to the church. Clearly issues of maintenance have their place, but they must always be subservient to the wider goals of the church. When Jesus gave the Great Commission, he did not say 'Keep the doors of my church open', but rather 'Go and make disciples' (Matthew 28.19). The agenda of the leaders' meeting must reflect the mission of the church. This means that items like membership, evangelism and social action should normally come at the top of the agenda. Leaders can then give their minds to the most important matters when they are feeling their freshest.

It is helpful if the agenda can be annotated, so as to enable leaders to give prayerful consideration to items before they come to the meeting. In this respect the recent custom of indicating the hoped-for outcomes is particularly helpful. For example, instead of just stating: 'Membership matters', the agenda might now read: 'Membership matters: to consider the applications of Bob and Sally'.

Relating to the wider Christian family

Inevitably the major items on any leaders' agenda will centre on issues affecting the local church. However, it is not right for any one particular church to live in isolation from others. Not only are we individually members of one another, individual churches are also members of a larger body (see 1 Corinthians 12). Leaders therefore need to ensure that the church is kept in touch with the wider Christian family. In the first place this might involve doing things with neighbouring churches, whether sister Baptist churches or churches of other traditions (e.g. the local group of Churches Together). In the second place, this will involve fostering relationships with such bodies as the local Baptist association, the Baptist Union and the Baptist Missionary Society. Although for Baptists it is the local church which is at the cutting edge of the Kingdom, nonetheless it is important that local churches do not become exclusively parochial in their vision. There is much to be said for wider issues of fellowship to be on the leaders' agenda at least once a quarter.

Leading the meeting

In many Baptist churches in the USA the pastor leaves the chair of the leaders' meetings to one of the other leaders. By contrast most British pastors prefer to take the chair and see this as being part of their leadership role, which involves actively guiding and encouraging the meeting along. To use the picture found in 1 Corinthians 12.28, the leader can be likened to a 'helmsman', who seeks not only to steer the ship but also to catch the wind of the Spirit in the sails. Hopefully most pastors have this spiritual gift of 'helmsmanship'. However, if there is another leader equally if not more suitably gifted, there is no reason in principle why that person should not chair. Clearly, where there is no pastor, somebody else has to chair. This may be the church secretary—but not necessarily. It is all down to gifting.

Exercising proper time-management

All too often one hears horror stories of leaders' meetings going on until midnight. But unless there is a particular crisis, this length of meeting is unjustified—and all the more so, when perhaps many of the leaders have the following morning to be out of the house by seven o'clock in order go to work. Meetings need to be limited. With good chairmanship and good organisation, leaders should be able to do their business in three hours. No meeting should be allowed to go on beyond 11.00 p.m. 10.30 p.m. should be the normal deadline! As Paul says in another context, 'the spirits of prophets are subject to the prophets' (1 Corinthians 14.32).

Praying at all times

'Pray without ceasing' (1 Thessalonians 5.17) wrote the Apostle Paul. Certainly it is vital that leaders' meetings are laced with prayer from start to finish. It is not sufficient to have prayer just at the beginning of the meeting, for at that stage the substance of many an item may be still unknown. Nor is it good to have prayer just at the end of the meeting, for by that time some may feel too tired to pray in a concentrated and adequate fashion. There is a lot to be said for having a major prayer-slot half way through the meeting. Needless to say, prayer doesn't have to be limited to the formal prayer-slots. When wrestling with a thorny issue, for instance, it can often be helpful to call a temporary halt to the discussion and ask the Lord for 'wisdom' (see James 1.5). It's amazing how often the way forward then becomes clear.

Almost inevitably, however, the time for prayer at leaders' meetings is limited. Somehow business tends to squeeze out time for concentrated prayer. Often the period for prayer gets reduced to ten minutes, if that. Hence it is good if leaders can make opportunities to meet together primarily for prayer. This could be of an evening. However, Saturday prayer breakfasts (e.g. from 8.00 to 9.30 a.m.) often prove more popular—not least because most of the day is still free.

Relating to the Church: An Ephesian Model

'There is one body and one Spirit, just as you were called to the one hope of your calling, one Lord, one faith, one baptism, one God and Father of all, who is above all and through all and in all.'
Ephesians 4.4–6

It is a truism to say that church leaders are only effective to the degree that they relate effectively to the church membership as a whole. For leadership to have any meaning, leaders have to work at their relationships with church members. Throughout this guide we have been looking at various specific ways in which leaders can serve their fellow church members. In this section we shall take a more general look at the way in which leaders might relate to the church, and in particular will seek to root our thinking in Paul's advice to the church at Ephesus.

Exciting fresh faith and hope in God

Effective leaders are visionaries, who have great faith and hope in God, and are able to communicate this faith and hope to the people in their charge. Christian leaders are great optimists, but optimists in the best sense of the word: suffering neither from false optimism, which ignores or dismisses problems, nor from pessimism, which allows people to be crippled by the problems that are around them, they see problems in the light of the God who 'is able to accomplish abundantly far more than all we can ask or imagine' (Ephesians 3.20). One of their key tasks is to enable God's people to see something of 'the immeasurable greatness of God's power' and to realise that it is available 'for us who believe' (Ephesians 1.17–19).

This communicating of the vision will at times take place on a one-to-one basis in private conversations. However, there will be other times when the vision is shared with the church at large. Leaders should not be afraid to speak out at church meetings, for they too are members. Particularly when a recommendation is brought from the leadership team, it is often helpful for a number of leaders to speak in its support. Yes, church members need to be allowed to have their say. But leaders are also called to give a lead.

Embracing 'love of another kind'

Effective leaders are so filled with 'the love of Christ that surpasses knowledge' (Ephesians 3.19) that they act as catalysts amongst the members to enable them in turn to love the unloving and the unloveable. God's love in Christ for his church—his agape-love (Ephesians 5.25,29)—is not just a model for relationships between husbands and wives, but for relationships in general. Leaders are to be to the forefront in living out, and encouraging others to live out, the injunction of Paul to 'Be kind to one another, tender-hearted, forgiving one another as God in Christ has forgiven you' (Ephesians 4.32).

Empowering for service

Effective leaders are in the business of enabling other members to fulfil their particular 'ministry' or service in the church (see Ephesians 4.12). Empowerment is the name of the game. One of their key roles is developing potential. In this respect leaders should always be looking to encourage, train up, and provide opportunities for the next generation of leaders.

Encouraging personal growth and development

Effective leaders are concerned to see not only the church but also individual members grow and develop in Christ (Ephesians 4.13–16). For this to happen they in turn need to be growing and developing themselves!

Serving with humility

There is no place for 'airs and graces' in church leaders. Leaders are not a different breed from other members: Paul's call to mutual submission (Ephesians 5.21) applies to them as much as to anyone else. Leadership may be a privilege, but it is not an honour. It is servant-leadership. No task is too small, no task is too menial. Humility should characterise servant-leadership, the kind of humility too which always recognises the worth of others and to acknowledge the mistakes of self.

Creating a positive climate

Effective leaders are positive and up-beat. There is no place for negativity and pessimism. Their concern is always for 'building up' (Ephesians 4.29) both individuals and the fellowship as a whole. When ideas are presented at the church meeting or elsewhere, they should always first be looking for the good in them—how might they work, as distinct from how might they fail. Such an attitude does not do away with a critical mind, and there are times when leaders need to encourage the church to say 'no'. However, it is all a matter of emphasis—about looking at the benefits first, and only then at the disadvantages. Rather than be Devil's advocates, leaders should seek to play the role of an Angel's Advocate!

Maintaining an open climate

Christian leaders are not the equivalent of MI5! Except where matters of confidentiality are involved, decision-making should always be made in an open manner. As 'children of the light' (Ephesians 5.8) we should not keep others unnecessarily in the dark. It is when the truth is spoken in love that the body of Christ is built up (Ephesians 4.15). Needless to say, the traffic should not all be one way. Leaders should also be able to consult and *listen* carefully to members, and take on board their concerns.

Praying for all God's people

Last but not least, Christian leaders pray for those in their charge (Ephesians 6.18). Christian leaders on a regular basis hold before God their brothers and sisters. Many find it helpful to work systematically through the church magazine or the weekly news sheet, the church handbook or the list of home group members. At the end of the day the system itself matters not—the essential point is that prayer is made.

AND FINALLY ...

'Keep watch over yourselves and over all the flock, of which the Holy Spirit has made you overseers, to shepherd the church of God that he obtained with his own blood.'

Acts 20.28

Throughout this book we have been thinking about the task of leadership. Yet, if leaders are to lead the people of God, they must in the first place be followers (John 20.19). Or as Paul put it to the Ephesian elders at Miletus: if they would care for the flock, they must in the first place keep watch over themselves (Acts 20.28). Leaders must never be so busy in the service of God that they never have time for God. If leaders would be men and women of God, then they must maintain the basic disciplines of prayer and of reading God's Word, as also of being in fellowship with all God's people.

It is in this context of leaders keeping watch over themselves that I offer a spiritual checklist. This could be a helpful exercise for a leaders' retreat, when it could be worked on first individually, and then the resulting thoughts and feelings shared with fellow leaders, who could then pray for one another. For, thank God, we are not called to walk the way of Christ alone, but rather together.

A Spiritual Checklist

My relationship with my Lord
1. Do I make time on a regular basis for private prayer and Bible study?
2. Am I truly sorry when I confess my sins? Do I 'mourn' over them?
3. Am I growing steadily?
4. Was I ever further forward than I am now?
5. Is there an area of my life over which Jesus is not truly Lord?
6. Am I filled with the Spirit's power?
7. Am I genuinely going 'all out' for Christ?
8. Do I delight to worship Christ?
9. Am I proud?
10. Am I aware of my gifts and am I using them for the Lord?

My relationship with my family
1. What am I like at home?
2. Is there anything concerning my behaviour at home of which I would be ashamed in company?
3. Do I love, comfort, honour and protect my partner?
4. Am I faithful to my partner in my thoughts as well as in my life?
5. Do I pray with my partner and share my deepest concerns?

6. Do I manage my children well?
7. What kind of spiritual lead do I give at home?
8. Do I have time for my family? Do I relax in their company?
9. Do I meet the needs of my parents?
10. Is our life together marked by the fruit of the Spirit?

My relationship with my fellow leaders

1. Do I pray for my pastor ever day?
2. Do I encourage my pastor?
3. Am I aware of any needs the pastor (and pastor's family) might have?
4. Is there any leader whom I fear, dislike, criticise or hold a resentment towards?
5. Are there any leaders and their partners whom I have not welcomed to my home?
6. Is there any leader whom I have not encouraged recently?
7. Do I keep confidences entrusted to me?
8. Am I reliable in carrying out the tasks my fellow leaders entrust to me?
9. When did I last encourage the leaders of organisations and activities in the church?
10. Can my fellow leaders count on me to pray through matters raised in earlier meetings of the leadership team?

My relationship with my church

1. Do I express love towards others in the fellowship?
2. Is there anybody in the fellowship I avoid?
3. Do I encourage others in the faith?
4. Am I loving enough to correct an erring brother or sister?
5. Do I make opportunities to pray with others in the fellowship?
6. Am I critical of others in the fellowship?
7. Is there anybody for whom I nourish an unforgiving spirit?
8. Do I pray for all the members of my house group?
9. Do I give generously to God's work?
10. Do I make an effort to get to know newcomers?

My relationships with 'the world'

1. Am I known as a Christian?
2. Am I seeking opportunities to build bridges of friendship with my non-Christian friends, neighbours and colleagues?
3. When did I last seek to share Christ with a friend, neighbour or colleague?
4. Am I praying for my non-Christian friends, neighbours and colleagues?
5. Do I get on with people in general?
6. Do I always speak the truth?
7. Am I a person of the strictest honesty?
8. Do I grumble or complain constantly?
9. Do I act like 'salt' in the world?
10. Do I keep up-to-date with the issues affecting my neighbourhood, town, country and world?

An Act of
Commissioning of Leaders

Statement of purpose

In the name of the Lord Jesus Christ we are now to receive and welcome these friends whom the Church Meeting has appointed to serve as leaders: ...

As servants of Christ in this church, they are called to [share with the minister in] the tasks of leadership and pastoral care. As a church we are called to trust them and pray for them, and at all times help them in the Lord.

The Lord Jesus said:
'Whoever wishes to become great among you must be your servant, and whoever wishes to be first among you be slave of all. For the Son of Man came not to be served but to serve, and to give his life a ransom for many'.

The Apostle Paul wrote:
'Having gifts that differ according to the grace given to us, let us use them: if service, in our serving; if leadership, with diligence. Do not lag in zeal, be ardent in spirit, serve the Lord'.

Question to the new leaders

My brothers and sisters, do you believe that God has called you through his church to serve in this role of leadership and pastoral care, and do you promise, with God's help, to exercise this ministry faithfully?

We do

Then we shall follow the example of the apostles and lay hands on you and pray for you.

Extempore prayer

In the name of the Lord Jesus Christ and on behalf of the church, I welcome you (back) to this office.

It is, however, not only leaders who are called to serve the Lord—every member of this fellowship has been gifted by God's Spirit with a view to Christian service. Let us ask God's help in fulfilling our varied callings as together we say the prayer of Ignatius Loyola.

(Responsive Reading *Baptist Praise and Worship* 422)

Congregational prayer

Teach us, good Lord, to serve you as you deserve:
to give and not to count the cost;
to fight and not to heed the wounds;
to toil and not to seek for rest;
to labour and to ask for no reward,
save that of knowing that we do your will. Amen.

A team covenant

I promise to:–
- Publicly communicate and support the decisions of the team
- Stay focused on the desired result even when problems occur
- Speak up when I dissent
- Do what I say I am going to do (no blinking!)
- Support my team colleagues, especially when I see them to be struggling
- Be ruthless about prioritisation
- Keep meeting-discipline
- Be ready to take risks, challenge conventional wisdom and learn from each other
- Listen to everyone's point of view
- Seek solutions, not problems
- Let others speak once before speaking twice
- Praise the achievements of others